I0625437

WHISPERS FROM THE HAZEL EYES

JAS SUNDARNATH

Copyright © 2023 Jas Sundar Nath

All rights reserved.

ISBN: 979-8-218-22823-1

No part of this publication be reproduced, distributed, or transmitted in any form or by any means, including photocopying, recording, or by any information storage and retrieval system, or by use of other electronic or mechanical methods, without the prior written permission of the publisher/author.

Printed in The United States.

Book cover design and illustrations by Jas Sundarnath.
Book cover design, Images and Illustrations created using Canva (www.canva.com).
Typeset in Baskerville Old Face and Garamond

First Printing, July 2023.

CONTENTS

ACKNOWLEDGMENTS

First, I want to thank God for giving me the gift of poetry and for always guiding me in my writing journey. I also want to express my deep gratitude to my parents, who have been my constant inspiration and support throughout my life. Their love and encouragement have made me who I am today. To my brother, thank you for always believing in me.

To my loving husband, thank you for your unwavering support and for always pushing me to be the best version of myself. You are my rock, and I love you more than words express. I could not have done this without you.

I want to extend my heartfelt thanks to my in-laws and extended family, who have always welcomed me with open arms and also for all of my friends who supported me in my endeavors.

To all the people from my past who have treated me with kindness, as well as those who have caused me pain, I thank you. You have taught me invaluable lessons about life and have helped shape me into the person I am today.

Lastly, I want to thank my future readers, who will be embarking on this journey with me. I hope my words touch your heart and soul and bring you the same joy and inspiration that authoring this book has brought me.

Thank you all from the bottom of my heart.

Sincerely,

JAS SUNDARNATH.

Whispers From the Hazel Eyes

HELLO

Greetings to you, my heart sings,

As if a thousand birds have taken flight...

A simple word, so small and sweet,

But it brought us together, in this cosmic feat...

You, my shining star in the sky,

Me, a humble soul, yearning to fly...

Our paths crossed, destiny played its part,

And all it took was a simple "hello" to start...

Your presence illuminates my life,

Like a beacon of hope in the darkest night...

I am in awe of your every move,

And my love for you continues to groove...

With you, I feel like I can take on the world,

My love for you forever unfurled.

As we journey together hand in hand,

I am grateful for that "Hello", a simple word...

EMBRACING EACH DAY

Each day that dawns before our eyes,

Is a precious gift, a grand surprise,

No matter what it may bring,

Be it joy, sorrow, or anything…

We must cherish each moment we are given,

And find the beauty that is hidden,

In the simplest things around,

Like the flutter of a butterfly's wings or the song of a bird's sound…

Every day is a journey we undertake,

A story we create with each step we take,

And though the road may be rough at times,

We must remember that our spirit still shines..

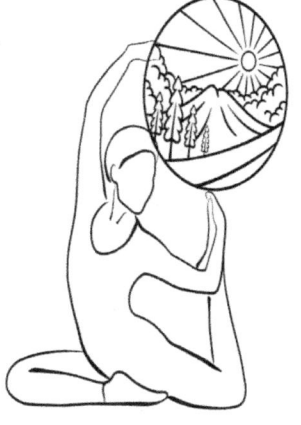

So let us embrace every single day,

And bask in the warmth of its golden rays,

For in every dawn there lies a chance,

To learn, to grow, to love, to dance…

[Cont'd…]

And when the day is done and night draws near,

Let us look back with a heart, which is clear,

Knowing that we have lived it to the best of our might,

And that tomorrow will be another day, shining bright.

THE BEAUTY OF NOW

The sky is a canvas of blue,

Fluffy clouds form shapes anew,

The sun plays peek-a-boo with the trees,

While the birds sing their melodies…

Sitting on a crimson bench,

A girl in a jean jacket drenches

Herself in the greenery around…

As the sun's warmth heals her runny nose, she's found…

At this moment she texts a friend,

While OneRepublic plays to no end,

Her lips wetted and her eyes aglow,

With the lyrics, she feels the flow…

[Cont'd...]

Her gaze falls on a lone bird high,

Flying aimlessly through the sky,

Just like her thoughts that have no direction,

Yet she feels no sense of rejection…

This moment with music and breeze,

As she witnesses the sunrise with ease,

Inspires her to write this poem anew,

To the very person she's thinking of, it's true...

RADIANT SOUL

A radiant vision caught on film,

An inspiration to all,

A symbol of what's possible,

A lady standing tall...

Born from love, a cherished daughter,

A sister with an open heart,

A daring adventurer, a loyal friend,

A blessing from the start...

We crossed paths, became friends,

Shared secrets, hopes, and fears...

Always comforting, encouraging, supporting,

Laughing through our tears...

[Cont'd...]

Today we celebrate the birth of a soul,

So full of love and light,

May your brilliance never fade,

And your spirit forever takes flight.

MY COFFEE TIME

Noises inside and out, disturbing my dream,

Hushed by my amor's smiling beam…

Opened my eyes to let the outside realm in,

Entering the coffee heaven is a world within…

Bubbling coffee took me to a memory,

Of hot springs in winter, oh so heavenly…

Smiling, my journey continued on,

With a song on the radio, my soul was drawn…

"Take me home, country roads," John Denver sings,

Humming along, my heart takes flight and wings…

Stepping out to the balcony, feeling free,

Taking in the beauty, a sight to see…

[Cont'd...]

There she stood, a royal mountain so tall,

In a gorgeous white snow saree, and glistening skin in thrall…

With her head held high,

Posing for a perfect picture, I can't deny…

The sun rises like a kid peeking behind his mother,

Her love is like green grass that stretches farther and farther.

Her kindness is like a cold breeze caressing my face,

A moment of bliss like a rainbow in its grace…

In all this chaos, I am thinking of my partner in crime...

Memories, moments, and my coffee time...

I smile and enjoy this blissful rhyme...

As I revel in this world so sublime.

FLIGHT OF THE BRAVE DOVE

The pure and gentle dove,

Robed in innocence and grace,

Bore a mark, a sign upon her back,

A trace of yellow, a mark of shame that none dared to explain...

But all beheld her beauty,

The golden freckles on her wings,

She took this as her due

And embraced her perceived blessings...

Yet her heart longed to soar,

To find her place, her destiny,

To take to the skies and explore

Beyond her flock's narrow decree…

[Cont'd…]

She left her home,

Soaring forth with dreams and hope,

But soon she found a world to roam

Where brutality and beauty interlope...

She flew to Eden's garden fair,

Trusting in its splendor and light,

But there she met betrayal and snare

And lost her faith in her hopeless plight...

With newfound wisdom as her guide,

She embarked to seek true love's light,

But on her flight, she found herself entwined

By hunger, pain, and violence that unkind...

[Cont'd...]

But she pressed on with fierce resolve,

Crossing oceans, lakes, and seas,

Enduring dangers that would devolve

The bravest of creatures with ease...

With night and winter closing in,

A weary dove sought refuge in snow,

Finding hope in melted ice akin

To the grace and mercy that does glow...

Yet, in the silence of the night,

She was ambushed by wolves so fierce,

With will and her spirit assessed, she must fight,

To escape their cruel and brutal pierce...

[Cont'd...]

In darkness and despair, she flies,

Her wings now wounded and bleeding,

Yet she perseveres, fueled by her heart's cries,

With flickering stars as her only guiding...

Finally, her journey's end draws near,

her white form covered in blood and bruise,

and she alights upon a shoulder dear,

finding solace and love with grace infused...

The pure and gentle dove has found

her purpose, her faith, her one true love,

and though her journey was fraught and profound,

she arose, guided by the heavens above.

HOPE IN THE DARK

Lost in the void of my emptiness,

I am swallowed by the blackness of distress...

The silence of the night echoes my pain,

A broken heart beating like an unsteady refrain...

A hollow emptiness calls out my name,

A siren's song that threatens to claim...

But I refuse to be swallowed by the night,

I refuse to give up without a fight...

For every day is a new chance to hope,

To break free of the cycle that feels like a rope...

To escape from the shadows that cling so tight,

And bask in the warmth of a guiding light.

[Cont'd...]

I know that somewhere there is a way,

A path to a better tomorrow and a brighter day...

I keep searching and keep moving forward,

With the hope that the future holds the best ahead...

Amid the darkness, I find my strength,

The power within me has breath...

To carry me through the toughest of nights,

And guide me to a life that's filled with light...

I hold onto hope with all my might

And push toward a future that's free of fright...

For even in the darkest hour hope shines through,

And helps me to find the strength to start anew.

DRESSING FOR THE NIGHT

As I sense the presence of someone passing by...

The wind whistles through the window frame,

And I feel a stir in my soul like a flickering flame...

As thunder rumbles in the distant sky...

There she stands, a queen of the night,

Her gown shimmers in the moon's silver light...

Her eyes, blue like the depths of the sea,

Beckon me forward to discovering what will be...

She takes my hand and leads me on a journey,

To a world beyond where magic is worthy...

In her wardrobe, I find a treasure trove,

Of dresses, each a story waiting to be told...

[Cont'd...]

With a smile, she whispers in my ear,

"Choose a dress, let it banish your fears...

With each garment, a new you shall appear,

Discover the magic, let it become clear."

I browse the dresses, each unique and rare,

And I feel a sense of wonder in the air...

Finally, I pick a dress that speaks to me,

A deep shade of blue, like the sea…

As I wore that dress, I feel a change inside,

New confidence, that I cannot hide...

The queen, my friend nods her head as if to say,

"Let your light shine like the stars on display."

I step out into the night feeling bold,

My heart flutters like a story to be told...

And as I move through the world, free and light,

I know the dressing for the night was right.

FAMILY BONDS BEYOND BLOOD

Beneath the roof of my second home,

Where love and duty interweave,

I strive to blend with the family

And earn the respect they once conceived...

The in-laws, a land uncharted,

A maze of customs and expectations,

With every step, I tread with caution,

Navigating through tricky relations...

My mother-in-law, a queen of the realm,

A matriarch with eyes that see through,

Her warmth and love, I feel so blessed,

A sanctuary in a world that is so new...

[Cont'd...]

My father-in-law, a stoic figure,

Whose words are pearls of wisdom,

With his guidance and support, I treasure,

A shield to protect me from the kingdom...

The family, a tapestry of hues,

A blend of personalities and ways,

In their love, I find comfort and refuge,

A home that grows dearer with each passing day...

Like a bird that takes flight to a new abode,

I've found a family that has embraced,

In their care and love, I've found a home,

A place where my heart and soul have been placed...

As a daughter-in-law, I may be new,

A branch that's grafted on a sturdy tree,

[Cont'd...]

But in their hearts, I know I have a place,

A family where I am loved and free...

And so, I blend my roots with theirs,

A bond that's strong and ever-growing,

With every passing day, I am grateful,

For a family that's kind, caring, and loving.

THE BRAVE GOLDEN DEER

In the woods, a deer ran wild,

But tiredness caught her in the night.

She drank from a pond and took some rest,

And woke up to find herself distressed...

A twig snapped and fear took hold,

But she pretended to be sleeping bold...

Her friends had turned into wolves,

And their laughter was far from good...

They spoke of her rare golden skin,

of tasting it and squeezing her thin,

Their cruel intentions she could not abide,

But the Brave Golden Deer fought to survive...

[Cont'd...]

She wept for help, strength, and grace,

And struggled to rise from her resting place…

She vowed to never give up the fight,

Even as her friends turned out to be a blight…

Nature saw her spirit within

And sent an elephant to save her skin…

Bruised, cut, and bloodied,

She survived; her strength embodied…

With her scars as her crown,

She spread hope to those who felt down…

A warrior, a queen, a shining light,

The Brave Golden Deer is an inspiring sight.

ENGRAVED IN HEAVEN

Life is fleeting like a passing breeze,

People come and go like leaves on trees...

They ask, "What will you take to the grave?"

I pondered, "Is it my identity that I save?"...

But is that all we are, a name, a label?

Etched on a tombstone, a fable?

Our true essence lies beyond this world,

In the deeds we've done and, in the love, we've unfurled...

For in the end, what remains of us,

Is not our possessions or earthly fuss...

But the way we've touched other lives,

With our kindness, our grace, our selfless ties...

[Cont'd...]

Let your light shine with righteousness and love

A beacon of hope sent from above...

May your kindness be like a flame in the dark,

Illuminate your path and leave a meaningful mark...

In the end, when our time is done,

Our identity is not lost but won...

Engraved in the heavens for all to see,

A legacy of love for eternity.

DIVINE RESCUE

Amidst the darkness, a secret plan was set,

To rescue and heal us from life's regret...

And suddenly a strong wind filled the room,

Whistling through the walls and dispelling the gloom...

The flickering flames that are shining bright,

Filled our hearts with a strange heat and light...

Melting away the hardness and coldness within,

Healing broken hearts, and restoring us from sin...

God's power struck our hearts ablaze,

And his son came to live inside our maze...

With an unbreakable love, he promised to stay

And guide us through life's uncertain way...

[Cont'd...]

No language barrier could stop the news,

Of the creator's love that's spreading like wildfire hues...

To villages, towns, and cities all over the world,

The family of God's children unfurled and unfurled...

And every day more and more believed,

In the love of God who never deceived...

Nothing in the world could stop his divine plan,

To rescue and heal us with his loving hand…

So, love God with all your heart,

He'll live inside you and never depart...

Guiding you, healing you, and setting you free,

In his divine rescue for all eternity...

SCATTERED LOVE NOTES

Love evoked,

Pain inflicted,

Insolence sting,

My shattered heart started aching,

By words made of dystopian daggers,

cerulean sobs,

eluded from my lips,

on a night of ivory silences…

when she found scattered letters...

The love notes…

EMBRACE YOUR WORTH

In this journey of life, you may encounter many doubts and fears,

But remember your worth is not defined by anyone else's sneers...

Your uniqueness is what sets you apart,

Don't let anyone dull your shine or break your heart...

Embrace your true self, flaws, and all,

For they make you stand tall...

No need to conform to society's standards or norms,

Your individuality is what gives you true form...

The road may be tough and the journey long,

But never forget that you are worthy and strong...

[Cont'd...]

So go ahead and chase your dreams,

Believe in yourself and all that you can be…

With every step, you'll discover more of who you are,

And soon enough you'll realize that you've come so far...

Embrace your true self for you are enough,

And don't let anyone tell you otherwise, be tough...

You are unique, you are special, you are one of a kind,

Embrace your worth and let your light shine.

WORDS UNSPOKEN

A pen in hand, I sit alone,

Yearning to unleash what I've never shown...

Breaking free from stifling thoughts,

Choosing words with care as each one is sought...

A need to express what's in my heart,

To share my feelings, not keep them apart...

With simple words, I hope to convey,

The depth of love that I feel each day...

No longer will I hold back or hide,

My true emotions are no longer denied...

My heart beats just for you, my love,

Together, we fit like a hand in a glove...

You make me whole, you make me complete,

Without you my world is incomplete...

Flying high, without wings or strings,

Together our love soars and sings...

[Cont'd...]

Your touch ignites joy within,

Unexplainable, but felt to the brim…

For all eternity, you'll be my one true love,

A gift from above, a treasure trove…

Zillions of words I keep within,

To express my love, but don't know where to begin…

Silence has now grown between us,

like a chasm we cannot cross…

ELECTRIC LOVE

In his presence, I found my peace,

His listening ear brought me to release...

He cautioned me with gentle care,

But my heart knew the love we share...

The vibe was perfect, the setting right,

Our souls ablaze, like a firelight...

The urge to touch and feel his skin,

A burning desire to let love begin...

Silently waiting to make the first move,

But at that moment our hearts did groove...

He turned to face me with a gentle shift,

My eyes gleamed like a moonlit drift...

[Cont'd...]

The urge to kiss overpowered our will,

Our lips met with a tender thrill.

Like a flash of lightning before the thunder,

Our love-struck with a passion for a wonder...

The world faded as we stood there,

Two hearts beating with a love so rare...

And in that kiss, we found our way,

Our love ignited like a bright display...

Like a flash of lightning that ignites the night,

Our love sparked with a soulful light...

And at that moment we knew for sure,

Our love was real and would endure.

PINK WINGS OF HOPE

In the sky so vast and blue,

A girl in pink takes flight anew,

The plane's engine roars and thrums,

As she sets off towards the sun...

With memories and thoughts in tow

And a heart that's anxious to know,

She's on a journey that's both exciting and new,

With so many questions and answers to pursue...

Her passion and zeal light up her face,

As she looks toward an uncertain place,

Her eyes hold both courage and fear,

As she takes a step toward what's near...

[Cont'd...]

She's on a path that's hers alone,

One that leads to the great unknown,

She's driven by devotion and love,

And a burning desire to rise above...

With every twist and every turn,

She's determined to learn and earn,

The success that awaits her at the end,

And the freedom that her wings can extend...

So, she flies high with braveness in her eyes,

And hope in her heart that never dies,

She's the girl in pink, soaring free,

On a journey to become all, she can be.

NEVER-ENDING JOURNEY WITH YOU

Met you and friendship bloomed

A bond that cannot be assumed

Sharing laughter, joy, and tears

The moments with you are cherished for years...

We've had our fights, and disagreements too

But I always made up and saw it through...

Promised to be there through thick and thin,

For you, I'll fight and always win...

Sometimes I've hurt you, and I'm sorry

I'll make it right, I won't tarry

Teased you, and you know it's in wholesome fu

But when I miss you, you are the one...

[Cont'd...]

The truth is, I'm always thinking of you

Every second, every minute, it's true

Can't imagine life without you near

You are valued and always so dear...

The journey with you is a long one indeed

But I know together we'll always succeed

In my thoughts, you'll forever be

My friend and my love for eternity...

LOST IN STRANGE LAND

In a land unknown,

I wander alone,

Lost amidst the hustle and bustle...

Of a people with hearts of steel...

Warriors, fighters, and strugglers all around,

Unknown looters lurking tall...

In a society where kindness does not abound,

And money is the ruler of all...

Racism and caste reign supreme,

Power is wielded by a select few in the regime,

In a world where the meek have no place,

And the powerful take what they desire in the race...

Amidst it all, I stand lost and alone,

Searching for a place to belong,

Yearning for a kindred spirit,

In this strange and unfamiliar land...

[Cont'd...]

Small acts of kindness, so rare and bright,

In a world where darkness is the only sight,

They give me the strength to continue,

To find my place, to belong...

And though the struggles may be great,

And the journey is long and hard to take,

I know I must persevere,

For I am not alone in fear...

There are others like me searching for a way,

To find a place in this land each day,

And together we will find our home,

A place of love where we'll never be alone...

So let us wander on with hope and grace,

Through this unknown and unfamiliar place,

For though the road may be tough to bear,

We'll find a way and we'll make it there...

[Cont'd...]

In this land unknown,

We'll find our way back home,

Through the darkness and the strife,

We'll carve out a path to a better life...

And when we've found our place at last,

We'll know that all our struggles have passed,

For in this land of heart and steel,

We've found a place where kindness is real.

NIGHTMARES

Under the darkening night, heavy rain pours down,

Rustling wind and scary demons surround,

In my dreams escape and rest are nowhere to be found,

As the lightning and thunder startle me with a deafening sound...

My eyes snap open from the grip of a nightmare's hold,

A shiver runs down my spine as chilling winds blow,

I'm grateful to have broken free from the terrors that unfold,

To embrace the comfort of the world once again, I know.

IN THE SHADOWS

I opened the window to let in some air,

But something else came and I was aware.

A chill in the air, and a sense of despair,

A presence unknown that caused me to stare.

Was it just a trick, or was it for real?

I couldn't tell, I didn't know what to feel.

The shadows moved just out of sight,

And the scent that filled my room was both eerie and light.

I felt exposed as they could see through,

Every fear and worry I held was so true.

I wanted to scream, run, and hide,

But the stranger outside wouldn't subside.

[Cont'd...]

The fear it instilled was truly surreal,

A sense of insecurity that I couldn't conceal.

I knew I had to act and close the window fast

Before the stranger's presence consumed me at last.

But still, the fear persisted and wouldn't go away,

And I wondered if the stranger was real, or just a play.

I was just imagining things,

But the fear I felt was still a painful sting.

So, I took a deep breath and faced my fear,

I knew it was the only way to clear.

I closed my eyes and opened them anew,

And realized that the stranger had disappeared without a clue.

Maybe it was all in my head,

But the fear it caused was not easy to shed.

I learned a lesson that we can face our fears,

And that they may not always be what they appear.

[Cont'd...]

Next time you see a stranger outside,

And you feel a sense of fear that you can't hide.

Remember to take a deep breath and be strong,

And know that the fear you feel won't last long.

DEATH OF A SECRET

In every heart lies a mystery untold,

A hidden gem, a story to behold...

Secrets we keep to protect, and hide,

For fear of judgment, shame, or feeling denied...

But the weight of secrets can be heavy to bear,

And the fear of judgment can lead to despair...

It's okay to seek a listening ear,

To share your secrets with someone near...

Some people will listen and care,

Who won't judge you or give you a stare...

They'll help you find the strength to break free

And guide you toward a path of honesty...

[Cont'd...]

For when secrets are shared and brought to light,

A weight is lifted, and the future seems bright...

New possibilities and chances arise,

And a burden is raised as the truth flies...

So don't be afraid to open up and confide,

In those you trust and who are by your side...

The death of a secret can led to new life,

And a chance to move forward without strife.

LOCKED IN A JAR

A strange dream came to me one night,

I woke up to a world that wasn't quite right,

My room was the same or so it seemed,

But I found myself in a place I'd never dreamed...

Outside the window, a goldfish swam,

But it looked like a whale in the ocean's expanse,

The aquarium was vast like the sea,

And I wondered what this could all mean to me...

I recalled a wish I made long ago,

To be hidden where no one could find me, so,

I could escape this life that's hard to bear,

But God had a different lesson to share...

[Cont'd...]

He granted my wish but, in a way, so strange,

He locked me in a jar far from my range,

To teach me to fight and never lose hope,

Even when I'm trapped, I must learn to cope…

God's humor may be peculiar and odd,

But the lesson he teaches is worthy of laud,

To keep fighting and never give in,

To survive anywhere, no matter how thin.

THE WEIGHT OF YOUR ABSENCE

Each day starts with a pang of ache,

As I wake up to an empty space,

Your side of the bed lies untouched,

Memories of your warmth are all I clutch...

I miss your voice, your touch, your scent,

The way you smiled, the way you bent,

To hold me close and kiss my cheek,

To tell me all the things you seek...

The world moves on, but I remain still,

Trapped in this void, against my will,

Your absence is a weight upon my chest,

Tearing me apart, my heart not at rest...

[Cont'd...]

I pray for strength to endure this pain,

To hold on to hope and to love again,

Till the day when we'll be together once more,

And my heart can finally heal and restore.

YEARNING FOR YOU

Relaxing alone on a bench in a serene place,

The aroma of roasted cashew nuts filled the space.

A strange feeling washed over me as I looked around,

A dark sky with shining stars and a white moon astounds me.

As I sat there, watching the stars twinkle in the sky,

Memories of you came flooding back, and I couldn't help but sigh.

I thought of the way your eyes sparkled in the moonlight,

And how your touch made my heart skip a beat, even on the darkest

night.

But now you're gone, and I'm left with this ache in my heart,

Wondering if we'll ever have a chance to make a fresh start.

I long to hear your voice, to feel your arms around me once again,

But instead, all I'm left with is this yearning, this endless pain.

[Cont'd...]

I try to distract myself with the music in my ears,

But even the love songs can't dispel my fears.

What if we never find our way back to each other,

And this longing, this emptiness, becomes mine forever?

And yet, I can't help but hold onto hope,

That someday, somehow, we'll find a way to cope.

That our paths will cross once again, and we'll be reunited,

And this yearning, this ache, will finally subside.

So, I'll keep on waiting, keep on dreaming,

Of the day when our love will be redeemed

And when our hearts at last beat as one,

This longing will have finally been overcome.

HEALING EMBRACE

Wrapped up in blankets, feeling so weak,

Feverish, and achy, barely able to speak.

My nose is stuffed up, and my throat is sore,

But in your arms, I don't mind it anymore...

Your touch brings comfort, a sense of ease,

As we snuggle together, you put my mind at ease,

Your warmth soothes my shivers as we lie here in bed,

I can't help but feel lucky to have you here instead...

We talk about anything and everything too,

Sharing moments, just me and you,

As I lay here sick, your presence brings light,

And in your embrace, I feel everything's all right...

[Cont'd...]

So, I'll hold on tight to this moment we share,

Wrapped up in blankets with you right there,

In sickness or health by my side, you'll be,

And that's all that matters, you're here with me.

SOUNDS OF SILENCE

Sounds of silence fill the midnight air,

And moonbeams dance upon the open sill,

A gentle breeze, a stillness rare,

As random thoughts fill my mind with a plan of will.

A rhythm or a tune, what do I hear?

The whistling wind or waves at sea?

But wait, more sounds, distinct and clear,

A knocking, a beat, a mystery.

Follow the rhythm, left, or right?

With each step, the sound draws near,

It's from the left that I have it right,

And now the thumps bring joy and cheer.

[Cont'd...]

The sound of silence, or so it seemed,

What do I hear? Are they my heartbeats, resounding true,

Once forgotten, now they're redeemed,

Renewed with hope and newfound excitement too.

My path of goals, of battles, I have won,

Of struggles faced and left behind,

Undoing nonsensical intentions, I've begun,

And a smile upon my face I find.

Dozing off with hope in my heart,

For a new morning and a fresh start,

A new me, ready to embark,

On a journey with a brand-new spark.

ALWAYS ON MY MIND

In every twinkling star that dots the midnight sky,

In every zephyr that gently brushes by,

In every moonbeam that floods my room with light,

You're always on my mind, day, or night...

When the sun's first rays herald the break of day,

When feathered friends take flight in cheerful play,

When leaves pirouette on the wind's whimsical sway,

You're always on my mind, come what may...

At the scent of a simmering dish of our favorite fare,

As I create something new with creative care,

When my pen flows freely and my thoughts take flight,

You're always on my mind shining bright...

[Cont'd...]

Whispers From the Hazel Eyes

When my heart races with passion or joy

When the distance between us seems to deploy

When my hiccups rise like ripples on a pond,

You're always on my mind forever bound…

No matter the miles that stretch out in between,

The connection we share is the strongest I've seen,

Our union burns bright like the stars in the sky,

And I'll keep thinking of you until the day I die…

Every thought, every feeling, every memory,

Makes the distance between us seem like a dream

As if someone was building a ladder from Earth to the sky,

Until the distance fades away, and you're forever by my side…

So, till that day, I'll keep you in my heart,

With every breath I take, I'll feel us never far apart,

In every moment of my life, I'll think of only you,

With every beat of my heart, my love is forever true.

WALK MY PATH

My path is like a rose with a stem of thorns,

At first glance, it may seem peaceful and adorned,

But it's not an easy climb to see the view,

There are hurdles to overcome to get to the truth...

The mountain of life is a sight to see,

An illusion of beauty that seems so free,

But to reach the summit, the journey is tough,

Hurdles await, and the wind is rough...

In the same way,

To know or see my inner beauty,

You need to know me,

Talk to me,

Befriend me,

Understand me,

[Cont'd...]

Feel my pain and troubles,

And the situation I went through,

And then put yourselves in my shoes,

And think how you might react at that point in time,

And above all to understand me completely in and out

For that you should be able to "WALK MY PATH".

BEING INSIDE A BAKING OVEN

I heard a girl's cries in the air,

Shouting out her pain and despair

I searched around, but no one was there,

Her whines continued echoing everywhere.

I followed the sound to an edifice building, so strange,

With walls that moved, a design so avant-garde.

A glass door is the only way to exchange,

With heat and pressure threatening to burn hard.

The girl was chained and trapped in the middle,

Her family, finances, and relationships are in a bind.

Academic and social pressures are like a hot kettle,

Burning her from below and above in kind.

[Cont'd...]

My heart ached, pain and heat all around,

Yet the girl fought and learned to persevere.

Unique solutions and ideas she found,

Breaking free from the chains of fear.

Like baking in an oven, she looked trapped inside,

But eventually, she learned to manage and thrive.

And then reality hit me, and I sighed,

It was just my past and my illusions that connive

My cake in oven was ready, and it was time to cool,

I decorated it with chocolate and gold,

Brightened sparkles brought joy and each piece of cake look so royal,

A sweet taste in our mouths, a moment to behold.

BLENDED EMOTIONS

In the mingling of light and shadow,

As the day fades into the night,

My heart is a blend of emotions,

A mix of hope and fright...

With the scent of spring in the air,

And flowers in full bloom,

I feel a blend of joy and wonder

And a sense of impending doom...

As I sit by the raging fire,

With the warmth of your love beside me,

I feel a blend of peace and passion

And a sense of swelling pride...

[Cont'd...]

In the rush of the city streets,

With the noise and chaos all around,

I feel a blend of excitement and fear

And a sense of being unbound...

Through the highs and lows of life,

As I navigate the twists and turns,

I feel a blend of all my feelings,

And a sense of gratitude that burns.

THE RAIN OF LOVE

In the journey of life,

People come and go,

Transient like passing clouds,

Some stay for a moment, others for a while...

But then, one day,

A cloud stops on your land,

And showers your garden with rain,

Each drop is like a seed of love,

Buried deep within your heart...

The seeds take root

And grow into saplings,

Budding into trees,

Bearing the sweetest fruits...

[Cont'd...]

The passing cloud persists,

Raining love, a ceaseless flow,

Nurturing the garden it assists,

Where love's tender blooms as bestow,

A forest of peace that everyone insists...

And someday, that sacred morn,

When clouds can hold back the rain no more,

The love you've fostered and borne,

boundless and pure,

Shall overflow into the world, touching the hearts at the core...

Then the love will be reborn.

SCORCHED MEMORIES

Memories-beautiful and unpleasant,

we etched in our minds,

And in a book of rustic pages,

I'd captured them in kind...

Every picture held a moment,

Every caption, a feeling well-spent,

But times, as they do, turned disastrous,

Misunderstandings formed, distance grew,

And lines became treacherous...

Overthinking bred a distance so vast,

Silence arrived, and communication

Became a thing of the past...

[Cont'd...]

Until one day, a note arrived,

Containing words that broke my soul,

made me feel deprived...

Tears filled my eyes, the emotions on overload,

Twitching hands and wobbling feet

as the weight of the words took hold...

And as I found my way to that rustic old notebook,

Anger rose inside me as rationality forsook...

As I flipped through the pages,

I found Memories scorched,

some partially burned, and others scattered all around...

But among the burned memories and scattered lines,

A glimmer of hope began to rise,

In those pieces, there's still a chance,

To rebuild, to restore the expanse...

[Cont'd...]

With determination, I gathered the fragments,

To mend what's broken and bring solace,

With love as my guide and forgiveness in sight,

I set out to make things right...

Each page became a canvas of hope,

Painted with understanding and scope,

Words of healing replaced the pain,

Breathing life into memories once slain...

Stitching the torn fragments together,

A tapestry of strength would gather,

In scars, there's hidden resilience,

A tale of growth, a powerful brilliance...

[Cont'd...]

With hope as my guide, I continue my quest,

To rewrite the chapters that were distressed,

In the darkness, the light will find its way,

To bring a brighter and more hopeful day...

As the final verse comes into view,

Life's poem carries on, steadfast and true,

Love, forgiveness, and hope we shall hold,

As we rewrite our story, creating new folds.

MIDNIGHT REFLECTIONS

Standing on the balcony, I gaze at the moon,

Wondering if there's someone out there who'll miss me soon,

My mind races with thoughts, insecurities, and fear,

Questions like, who am I important? start to appear...

As the moments pass, my tears start to fall,

And I'm left feeling lost and so exceedingly small,

I hope someone will message or call out my name,

But the silence is deafening, and nothing's the same...

The thunder roars and lightning fill the sky,

I feel its energy and it seems to say, "Don't cry",

The rain starts to pour and caresses my face,

Bringing comfort and solace in this lonely place...

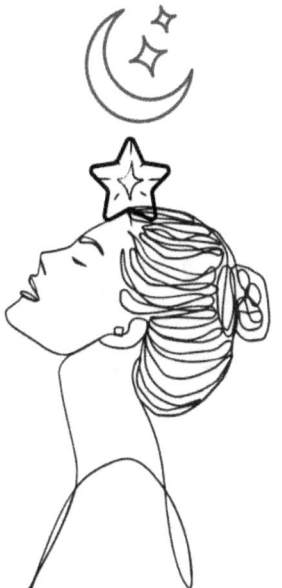

[Cont'd...]

As the rain ends, and the sky clears up,

I close the door and hold my head up,

I thank God for what I have and for the rain,

Took a deep breath, and tried to ease the pain…

I'm still a broken girl with doubts and fears,

But with faith in my heart and a smile through tears,

I'll face the struggles and battles in my mind,

Knowing that I'm not alone and a better future I'll find.

WILL I EVER BE FREE?

I thought I was free,

To chart my course at sea,

But fear and doubt's chains, tight around my heart,

Casting shadows that linger, tearing me apart...

Capturing my spirit and conquering my soul,

I'm reduced to a puppet, a mere funny role,

Trapped and tangled into a mortal marionette,

Playing a part, I am hoping to forget...

How can I break free?

From this weight that burdens me,

Lost in a sea of uncertainty,

Will I ever find the key?

But then I remember,

[Cont'd...]

Will I Ever Be Free?

With God's grace by my side,

I'm not weak or frail,

Hope is my guiding ember,

That can make my courage prevail...

I'm the captain of my fate, guided by the divine,

And the captain of my soul's design,

I'll let go of these chains of hate,

And take back control as God aligns.

MY SAGA OF LOVE

An adventure of the battles, fought by me,

Returned with scars, sometimes won, sometimes lost,

My heart craved love, love, and love,

Till it got shattered into pieces.

It is more than just loss and tears,

My saga of love was never revealed,

I buried it within and hid it,

Afraid of what the world might say,

But now I am ready to let it out

And share my truth, come what may.

Love is worth the risk and pain,

And though it may bring hurt and strife,

The joy it brings is worth the cost,

And love makes it all worth the fight.

[Cont'd...]

I stand here, bold, and true,

With my heart worn on my sleeve,

I'm ready to face whatever comes,

And finally, let my feelings be free.

I LOVE YOU

In a world so uncertain and vast,

I discovered a love that makes time stand fast.

You're my sun, bringing warmth and light,

Guiding me like the moon on the darkest night.

With you, my smile never fades,

Even through trials and escapades.

You make my heart dance and leap,

Each word you utter is so captivating and deep.

Your love flows through me like a gentle stream,

A rhythmic melody, a cherished dream.

Every moment spent with you I treasure,

Grateful to the stars for this beautiful pleasure.

[Cont'd...]

Tomorrow's mysteries remain unknown,

But with you, I never feel alone.

You complete me in every single way,

And my love for you grows with each passing day.

EMBRACING LIFE'S CHALLENGES

Life is full of twists and turns,

And sometimes it can be tough to discern,

But when you face a challenge, don't be concerned,

For there's a lesson to be learned...

It's easy to dwell on what's gone wrong,

But it's better to focus on being strong,

And use your challenges as a steppingstone,

To reach new heights that you've never known...

When things don't go according to plan,

Remember that you're not alone,

And with time, you'll understand,

That life's challenges can be overcome...

[Cont'd...]

So, when you face a tough situation,

Don't give up or give in to frustration,

Instead, face it with determination,

And see it as an opportunity for personal transformation…

Because when you overcome life's obstacles,

You'll come out stronger and more capable,

And you'll be ready for whatever life throws your way,

With a newfound sense of strength every day.

FAMILY TREE

Beneath the sheltering family tree,

I stand, watching leaves sway gracefully,

With every breeze, whispers unfold,

Tales of our ancestors, the stories untold.

My mother is the guardian of our home,

Nurturing and caring for the home from strife,

My father is both the provider and protector,

Guiding us through each step-in life…

My brother, my ally, and my friend,

Together we climb the branches and play,

With every moment that we spend,

Our bond grows stronger each day…

Family Tree

[Cont'd…]

The children, the promises of the future,

Buds on the branches, full of glee,

Growing, exploring, becoming mature,

With each passing year, they become the tree...

Our family name, our tribe, our kin,

A legacy cherished, passed from within,

A tree with roots that reach far and wide,

Enduring storms, faith is never denied.

As a cherished daughter, I am a branch,

Nurtured by love and family, an eternal bond,

United we stand, mighty and strong,

Thriving for generations as our legacy prolongs.

ECHOES OF LOVE

Like a melody that lingers on,

Your memory stays with me all day long.

Thoughts of you, they dance and play,

In my mind, they never fade away...

Your laughter echoes in my soul,

A symphony that makes me whole.

Every moment we shared is a treasure,

A priceless gift, beyond all measure...

As time goes by and we grow old,

These memories will never grow cold...

They'll keep us warm, through storm and strife,

A constant source of love and life...

[Cont'd...]

Like echoes, they bounce and rebound,

Our love will resound, all around...

In every heart and every place,

The echoes of love will never fade...

THE DREAM I DREAMT IS OF YOU

In my dreams, I find myself in a world of bliss

A place where all my worries cease to exist

And in this world, you are always by my side

As I dream of you, my heart fills with pride…

Your presence brings calm to my restless mind

And all my troubles, to you I can confide

In this dream world, I relive our memories so sweet

And the love we share is ever so complete…

Though in reality, we may be miles apart

In my dreams, you're always close to my heart

I love to dream of being the one you adore

And in my dream world, we'll love each other more...

[Cont'd…]

So let my dreams be my happy place

Where I can always see your loving face

In my dreams, you're my heart's desire,

And with you, my dreams will never expire.

THE BREATH OF TIME

A moment suspended in time,

As the gentle breeze caresses my mind,

Thoughts swirl like leaves in the wind,

As the sun sinks low, the day comes to an end...

I wait with bated breath and heart ablaze,

For the one I cherish, my heart's secret maze,

To step into the glow, which is radiant and true,

And ignite my soul, a flame that pierces through...

The world around me fades away,

As I drink in the sight of my love today,

A smile on their lips and a twinkle in their eye,

I feel my spirits lift and I cannot

lie...

[Cont'd...]

We talk, we laugh, we share our dreams,

And time flows by like a gentle stream,

At that moment, everything is alright,

And I know with certainty, love is in sight...

But as we part ways, I feel a tug,

A reminder that life is never snug,

That the wrong path can feel so right,

But true happiness is worth the fight...

So, I hold on tight to what I know,

That love is the river that makes life flow,

And every moment we share is a gift,

This is a reminder that time is short and swift...

So let us cherish every breath we take,

And let love guide us through every turn we make,

For, in the end, it's the love we give and take...

That makes life a journey, we will gladly undertake.

UNVEILING THE PHOENIX WITHIN

In the depths of despair, she found her way,

A resilient soul, with strength on display.

Through trials and turmoil, she faced every fray,

Emerging triumphant, brighter each day.

Once wounded and broken, a spirit confined,

She rose from the ashes, leaving the pain behind.

With a fire within, she forged a new mind,

Determined to thrive, her purpose defined.

Molested and scarred, her innocence was lost,

But deep in her heart, resilience was embossed.

She refused to let the price define her

and at all cost, she recovered back her power.

[Cont'd...]

Heartbreak's bitter sting and tore her apart,

Yet piece by piece, she mended her heart.

With unwavering courage, she'd make a fresh start,

Turning pain into wisdom, a work of art.

Family struggles weighed heavy on her soul,

But she stood tall, determined to make it whole.

Through love and forgiveness, she took control,

Creating a future where happiness would enroll.

In the ashes of a broken marriage's flame,

She found the strength to break free from the shame.

Unshackled, she rose, embracing her name,

Transforming her scars into sources of fame.

Rumors and whispers, like venom they spread,

But she paid no mind to the lies people said.

For she knew her worth, and with grace, she tread,

Leaving behind the falsehoods, her spirit unwed.

[Cont'd...]

Now she stands before you, reflecting a new light,

A holder of knowledge, her mind shining bright.

Through trials and tribulations, she never shies from a fight,

Fulfilled goals while setting new heights.

A poet, her words dancing on the page,

Crafting stories of resilience, hope, and change.

With her first book blooming in a literary stage,

She inspires others, igniting their own sage.

To her older self, she speaks with affection,

"I've triumphed through the darkness, defied imperfection.

With courage as my compass, I've found my direction,

A warrior, survivor, filled with introspection."

So let her story inspire, a testament true,

That even in darkness, the light breaks through.

No matter the struggles, the battles she knew,

She emerged as a victor, and so can you.

TILL DEATH DO US APART

With every breath I take, I think of you,

Without you, I'm lost, and don't know what to do,

Thoughts of you are always on my mind,

Wishing you were here, so close to find…

My heart aches for your tender touch,

And the warmth of your love that I miss so much,

I close my eyes and see your face,

And feel the emptiness in this lonely space…

The distance between us makes me cry,

But the thought of being with you makes time fly,

Your love brings me bliss and keeps me going,

And your words of comfort keep me glowing…

[Cont'd…]

Your eyes sparkle like the stars above,

And your smile fills my heart with love.

I can't wait to hold you close and tight

And kiss you with all my might…

In celebration, we merge traditions rare,

A testament of love, a bond we declare.

Among the challenges of life,

With love, we learnt to survive…

One day the marriage of hearts took place

Among all the odds we both found our solace…

Proven that by divine grace a wedding of love stays so strong,

Till death do us apart, inside your heart is where I belong.

FREEDOM

Through the waves, we swim,

Amidst forests, we roam,

Risking all we have,

To find a place called home.

But true freedom,

Is found in the One above,

Who gave His life to save us

And showed us how to love.

Amidst the noise we hear,

The world claims joy is near,

But only in Christ, we find,

A joy that's real and dear.

Strategies and weapons were made,

The research was done, and battles played,

Yet freedom seems far away,

Until in Christ, we find our way.

[Cont'd...]

We fight for dreams and rights,

Sacrificing days and nights,

But true freedom is not found,

In earthly dreams that abound.

Face your battles with grace,

In Christ, we find the strength to face,

A life of freedom and joy,

As we follow His path with poise.

Stay happy and stay true,

In Christ, we are made anew,

Spread His love and shining light,

To those who need it most, in sight.

Until the day death comes,

We'll keep shining like the sun,

For those who believe in Christ,

True freedom has just begun.

[Cont'd...]

For death is not the end,

But the beginning of a life that's grand,

As we enter His eternal presence,

And live in His love forevermore, hand and hand.

ABOUT THE AUTHOR

Jas Sundarnath is an industrial engineer and poet from Hyderabad, India, currently residing in Utah, USA. She holds a bachelor's degree in Computer Science from INDIA and a master's degree in Industrial Engineering from New Mexico State University. Jas has been writing poetry since her undergraduate days and her debut poetry book, "Whispers from the Hazel Eyes," is a compilation of some poems that she has written over the years till today.

This debut poetry book is a collection of raw and emotional poems that explore themes of love, loss, and healing. Jas's writing is inspired by her struggles and experiences. Writing has been her way of coping with her emotions and finding solace in challenging times. She hopes that her poems will resonate with readers who are going through similar challenges.

Jas's writing style is characterized by vulnerability and honesty, and she often writes about topics of romance, heartbreak, and self-discovery. She draws inspiration from her life experiences including her marriage to her husband, who encouraged her to publish this book. As an Indian woman living in the United States, Jas is enthusiastic about sharing her unique cultural perspective with readers around the world.

Jas shares her poetry on her Instagram page, @jas_s.poetry, where readers can connect with her and stay updated with her writing. When she's not writing, Jas enjoys playing badminton, gardening, and watching movies. She is also an avid reader of poetry and romance fiction and draws inspiration from her favorite authors and poets.

Jas hopes her book will encourage others to share their stories and find hope and healing through writing.

MY PERSONAL LETTER TO EACH READER

Dear Readers,

I want to take a moment to express my heartfelt gratitude for joining me on this poetic journey. Your presence and support mean the world to me, and I am genuinely thankful that you have chosen to delve into the pages of my poetry book. As you read these verses, I hope they resonate with the depths of your soul, awakening emotions and sparking reflections.

I encourage you to share your thoughts and reviews about the book on the website you buy or on my Instagram page with permission to share it online to many other readers, as your feedback is invaluable to me. Your stories and experiences are a source of inspiration and connection, and I would be honored to be your listener, ready to embrace the tales that have shaped your own unique journey.

May God's blessings be upon you, illuminating even the darkest corners of your life with a glimmer of hope. May you walk a path filled with kindness, compassion, and unwavering optimism. Remember that you are never alone, for the divine presence surrounds you, guiding and supporting you through every step.

Thank you for being a part of this beautiful journey. May your life be blessed with endless possibilities, and may you always find solace, inspiration, and joy in your faith and this beautiful world around you.

With heartfelt appreciation and prayers,

Jas Sundarnath.

www.ingramcontent.com/pod-product-compliance
Lightning Source LLC
Chambersburg PA
CBHW060332130626
46553CB00003B/982